LOST POEMS

MATTHEW RASNAKE

JETPACK WANDERER PRESS

lost poems © 2020 by Matthew Rasnake

All Rights Reserved. No part of this book may be used or reproduced, stored or transmitted, in any form or by any means, electronic, material, visual, audible, or otherwise, without written permission from the author, except in the case of brief quotations embodied in critical articles and reviews or under the doctrines of fair use. For information, contact the author at PO Box 5143, Louisville, KY 40255

Publication Note:

The poems in this collection were written in the nearly two decades between 1991-2009.

Several (twenty-two) of the poems included here were previously published in the Christ of my Confusion, *which had an initial limited hand-bound edition of twenty numbered copies, and a subsequent 50-copy limited professional printing.*

First Edition

ISBN: 978-1-7360856-0-8

Library of Congress Control Number: 2020922315

Jetpack Wanderer Press
Louisville, KY

For Sara, who saved me.

CONTENTS

Preface	vii
PEOPLE AND SOCIETY	**1**
afterthought	3
melting pot	4
not going our way	5
small talk	6
drenched in ignorance	7
I hate people	8
politics & pageantry	9
bullshit	10
12 year-old drunk	11
with a glance	12
she walks in	13
STRUGGLE AND SORROW	**15**
fallen	17
chances	18
confusion	19
playing the game	20
get on with it	21
reflections	22
off	23
no meaning	24
always me	25
don't try	26
I try to speak	27
runaway	28
remembering	29
too much coffee	30
tired	31
sleepless	32
torture the soul	33
why	34
the heavy air	35
falling apart	36

PAIN AND DEATH	37
money for food	39
perfectly happy	40
cross eyed world	41
mortality	42
the mood strikes	43
existence is pain	44
I wish I could	45
JOY AND LIFE	47
the fear of God	49
anticipation soars	50
no direction	51
driving through the night	52
Hardee's coffee	53
holy ground	54
coffee shop world	55
manic	56
literati	57
drunken poetry	58
overthrow	59
return to imperfection	60
on edge	61
the path	62
the world opens	64
time	66
now is the time	67
invisible phantoms	68
in the house of a stranger	69
what is left to write	70
her voice resounds	71
beyond	72
Acknowledgments	73

PREFACE

It is a strange thing, to revisit—decades later—a decade's worth of feverish creative output. For me, there's an ongoing battle between my compulsion to produce something from and my doubts about the continued relevancy of past work.

It is, therefore, both gratifying and maddening how well some of these old yawps of Id and Ego reflect a present world that has apparently not learned from past mistakes. I wrote most of them as a twenty-something small-town kid who'd only just begun to grow past his boundaries. And now kids—like I was then—are smashing through supposed boundaries like rice paper. It's breathtaking to watch.

Life holds space like a chasm between now and then that yawns open until vertigo takes hold. It's astonishing how much has changed—and changed me with them. It's an admonition how much hasn't.

And yet we're all human. No matter the gross nature of our individual existence, we all—if we're lucky—get annoyed, confused, wound up, angry, hurt, doubtful, scared, elated, loved, hopeful. We can—if we make the effort—all see ourselves in others. We can—if we're open enough—all stand up and accept the strengths and weaknesses, the similarities and differences that make us all part of our vibrant, diverse human community.

I'm not trying to suggest that this book represents some profound work of human compassion, but maybe, if I'm lucky, you'll see for a moment that what I've said here is true. We're all different, but we're all the same, and we're all in this together.

LOST POEMS

PEOPLE AND SOCIETY

LOST POEMS

afterthought

>small
>a tiny being
>an addition to
>the life on the streets
>an afterthought
>placed without purpose
>observed & yet unseen
>noticed & yet unknown
>
>glances of contemptuous
>disdain
>from pockets of moving
>humanity
>unconcerned for the world
>around them
>concerned only for themselves
>
>they see me as they see
>a wad of chewing gum
>used up & discarded
>on the walk
>to be sidestepped & ignored
>and forever forgotten

melting pot

>
> CAUTION
> CUIDADO
> multi-lingual wet floor sign
> in the heart of America
> they pour in every day
> people
> in search of freedoms
> that just don't exist
>
> America
> land of the free
> home of the brave
> land of opportunity
> land of bullshit
>
> cum-splattered wife-battering politicians
> rule the land
> a melting pot of humanity
> but the heat's way too low
>
> separation segregation pain and hate
> are the masters here
> lies and liars in a land of people
> who can't hear the truth
> and wouldn't care if they could

not going our way

    Mountain Dew
    mmmm
    tasty beverage

    corned beef &
    sauerkraut sandwiches
    on the corner of the world
    fill my belly with
    warmth and
    creamy cheesy goodness

    all the little people
    come in and go out
    with their little worlds
    and a Phil Collins soundtrack

    the rainbow streets flow
    following predetermined
    patterns,
    sure we're
    going where we want,
    but we're
    not going our own way

    how can anyone be happy
    in this world of condos & convents
    no one living by their own will?

small talk

    sitting in the early morning sun
    hot yellow light warm on my back
    my body cold
    in the chill breeze
    of a late November day
    pale blue sky
    full of shadowy clouds
    wispy strings of smoke
    in the heavens
    the breeze blowing in my ear
    overpowers the conversations
    subjugates the words of those around me
    chattering people
    carrying conversations of meaningless words
    small talk
    saying nothing

LOST POEMS

drenched in ignorance

    futile worthless discussion searing
    professor speaks with tongue of lead
    students with their dumb ears hearing
    watch the clock with lessening dread

    mumble bumble nimbly say
    words from thoughts tumble through
    striking teeth & tongue along the way
    intelligence not from ignorance spew

    not-bright questions quickly asked
    feeble half-truth answers falter
    poor my brain in dim light basks
    drenched in ignorance from the fodder

I hate people

>   I hate people
>   I've never met
>   a leer
>   a look
>   an attitude
>   displayed
>   by puffed chests
>   squared shoulders
>   and hard eyes
>
>   cold looks
>   above patronizing smiles
>   fake laughter
>   sends cheese grater chills
>   up my spine
>   stupid people
>   with something against the whole world
>   who think everyone owes them
>   something
>   because they were born
>
>   clueless morons
>   unwilling to accept their inferiority
>   and trying to cover it
>   with posturing
>   and false intelligence
>   and by preying on
>   ones who see their attempts
>   as sincere

politics & pageantry

>politics & pageantry
>half-hearted smiles
>full of teeth
>cold handshakes
>& hard hearts
>unknown & unknowing
>not listening and trying
>to communicate

bullshit

>
> BULLSHIT
> I hate bullshit
> in any form
> from anyone or anything
> there is so much
> from the government
> from society
> from individuals
> it makes me cringe
> govnt for the people
>
> Natnl Guard bullshit
> let's go to the woods
> set up a tent go to sleep
> take it down clean it up
>
> it's ALL Bullshit
>
> people accept it
> people deny it
> people try to explain it
> but there are no explanations
> it's bullshit
>
> budgets
> schedules
> taxes
> dress codes
> appearance regulations in the work place
> **BULLSHIT**

12 year-old drunk

> little young stupid punks
> obvious products of the MTV
> young adult factory
> lamenting the death
> of one their own age
> 12 year-old drunk sitting
> smoking a cigarette
> talking to me about someone
> I never knew
> and will never know
> as if I care
> maybe it's better for them
> to taste their mortality
> so early in the game
> or maybe it will only enforce
> their MTV education
> that stupidity is good and
> death makes you famous
> and not to be forgotten

with a glance

> your sensuous ways
> are somehow familiarly foreign to me
> like an old language
> spoken by a grandparent
> but never learned
> your beautiful eyes
> deeply expressive
> are capable of conveying or hiding
> your innermost thoughts and desires
> with a glance

she walks in

> she walks in
> just as I imagined she would
> & I sit
> I briefly look up and smile
> and continue writing
> I tap my ashes and sip my coffee
> hardly looking at her
> she sits across from me
> as I finish the poem
> and say hello
> we chat briefly about nothing
> idle talk
> and then we go
> to continue the charade
> in another location

STRUGGLE AND SORROW

fallen

    my angel has fallen
    my godhead destroyed
    things I held high
    lie on the ground
    my tired arms have folded
    and my fantasy has crashed back
    under the pressure of reality

    my nightlight has dimmed
    my flashlight is dead
    there is nothing to guide me
    through the darkness of the world
    the darkness of my life
    the darkness

chances

everything in life is ruled
by chance
nothing can be determined
nothing can be planned
nothing can be counted on
we give & take chances
some work out
some don't
there are times though
when we've given too many
& have to take our own
times when one more chance
must be the last

it's too late
been too long
said too much
didn't achieve enough
it's over
it's done

LOST POEMS

confusion

clouds in brain
like cobwebs
in an old forgotten
corner of an attic
in an abandoned house
thoughts
once straight
now cross in my head
like happy-go-lucky clowns
laughing at me
behind my back

what to do
what not to do
life decisions to be made
but not presenting themselves
for close inspection

do I leave
or stay
do I love
or hate
do I work
or play

and how do I know
if any decision I make
will be a correct one?

playing the game

what will you do
what should you
in this game
of life
rolls of the dice
or spins of the wheel
just can't cut it
each piece
can move in infinite
directions
and the steps
on the path to success
aren't laid out
or known
beforehand

get on with it

    things in life are seldom clear
    choices never as easy as this or that
    every action carries a certain weight
    every one thing effects another
    why can't things be easy
    why must life be so tough
    why can't we bypass the bullshit
    and get on with it

reflections

    standing alone in the half-light
    reflections on window in the dark
    looking at the shadow of a man
    staring back deep into my eyes
    I see myself
    and yet I cannot
    I want to see myself
    as others see me
    as others think of me
    I want to know what words
    spring into the minds of those around
    when they see the big man walking

    I want to know myself as others know me
    I want to stand off from myself
    and be able to hear my voice
    as I, joking, laugh at myself
    in the night

    what is me
    who am I
    how can I find myself

    in this world of
    thinly-veiled half-dark
    representations of the inner self
    step out from the body
    and perceive with the
    virgin eyes of a new acquaintance or
    the hardened view of an old friend.

    who was I
    who am I yet to become
    and how am I approaching
    he who is
    and will be
    me?

off

I have lost my center
that inner being which drives me
that chaotic core which guides me
motivation is low
inspiration fleeting
things I see & feel are less
experience is dulled
drained of life to the bare facts
little substance remains
of a full life
lived to the fullest
and unrealizing its potential
ideas and plans lie tickling
at the back of my brain
to be released
but never
things to do
never to be done
my soul obscured by a gray cloud
through which I cannot see tomorrow
and sorrow fills the laughter
of my conscious dreaming
pains tells of the health of the body
and anger screams of unanswered love

no meaning

I live my life
in a daze
sleeping only
between the dreams
nothing I do seems real
there's no purpose
no meaning
to give life
substance
everything I see or touch
is like a shadow
nothing I taste or smell
satisfies my
appetite

always me

    these conversations
    are all so familiar
    but it was so long ago
    the memories are hazy
    dredging up parts of my past
    I don't care enough about
    to think of

    I exist here
    in this time
    this place
    I've always been here
    I've never been somewhere else
    the locations change
    but I'm always me
    I can't be anything
    or anyone else

    I'm always me
    but I'm always changing
    always adding experiences
    knowledge
    always losing some old memory
    losing my mind
    leaving things behind
    going to what's ahead
    heading towards
    what will be
    me

    eventually I'll meet myself
    and then I'll know
    why these conversations
    seem so familiar

don't try

    no matter what
    don't try
    to change
    don't try
    to make a difference
    don't try
    to get ahead
    don't try
    to be happy
    don't try

    'cause it won't work

    if you try to break even
    you'll end up broken
    if you try to rise above
    you'll fall that much farther

    if the end of your trouble is near
    don't run
    if you see the light
    don't look
    if you find a solution
    don't think
    it'll make anything
    better

LOST POEMS

I try to speak

> I can't get a word in
> and wouldn't want to
> when I try to speak
> intelligently
> it comes out wrong
> stupid
> my tongue trips
> the words fall flat
> my lips close
> and what I want to say
> has no outlet

runaway

    is this my lot
    to never know
    for sure
    to never connect
    to be forever
    alone
    with the night
    and a knife

    hey, I've tried
    don't think I haven't
    it just doesn't seem
    to work

    I sit down
    I stare at you
    I can't think of anything to say

    I've got no reason to stay
    so I run

    and I still don't know
    who you are
    or who I am
    or why
    it even matters

remembering

>if only I could forget
>that memory is faulty at best
>and at worst,
>what?
>
>blurred blued images of time
>remind me of things past
>long forgotten
>still not remembered
>
>I see half parts and pieces
>of things which occurred
>and yet did not
>things I can't remember with the clarity
>I wish for
>
>to remember every detail
>to see faces
>to hear words
>spoken from lips
>long closed and gone
>
>to feel the essence of emotions
>that clouded my brain
>against the backdrop of time
>
>but I cannot
>
>I am a deaf mute
>in a world of sights and sounds
>a rock in a world of emotion
>seeing nothing
>hearing nothing
>feeling nothing

too much coffee

    this monkey
    on my back
    keeps getting bigger
    he keeps wrapping
    that damn tail
    'round my neck

    I find it hard
    and harder to breathe
    each day
    something's gotta give
    maybe I'm just overexcited
    & worked up
    over nothing

    maybe I've just had
    too much coffee…

tired

    red-rimmed eyes
    uncontrollably squinting
    loose lids
    scratch
    dry eyeballs
    blinking
    small scale
    violence
    driving away
    consciousness
    and sleep
    that won't come
    anyway

sleepless

    I cannot sleep
    in the night I toss & turn
    my eyes flutter and squint
    to ward off light that is not there
    I try hard as I can
    to relax, let go, lose myself
    to the specter, sleep
    but it doesn't help
    I can't eat
    not as I used to
    I eat small meals that fill me
    but do not quench my appetite
    I am exhausted
    constantly now, activity is
    more difficult
    I yawn & grumble & groan & creak
    with the weight of my body that is nothing but
    mental?
    the world is slower, smaller
    and yet more dazzling & abstract
    and still boring
    I see it as never before
    all shapes and colors
    rough blobs of existence
    moving about a dull lifeless landscape
    I see joy & rage & peace & hope & pain
    in eyes that wander and dart
    darkly about
    I see in many the war
    between teeth and lips
    as the white tries to show through
    the constricted red
    in a play of happiness
    which doesn't show
    in the eyes

torture the soul

    I can't see with open eyes
    blind
    broken
    the answer is in front of me
    but I can't remember the question
    everything is different, changed
    visions are heard
    and sounds are seen
    as murals on dark walls
    hidden
    I can feel the air, the ground
    but when I look
    it's gone
    I can feel your eyes on me
    when you're not there
    it's time to stop
    go back, turn around
    but I can't
    I can't listen to myself
    or the others
    telling me what to do
    I can't listen
    have to keep going
    keep thinking, feeling
    hurting
    I lash myself with thoughts
    and my back is striped
    red with anger
    my eyes close
    and bat
    and blink
    torture the soul
    to think
    think
    what
    no… it's nothing.

why

what the hell are you talking about?
if you know so much
why do you sound so unconvincing
for every question you have an answer
for every point you have a counter
how did you get so wise
how did you come by this knowledge
how is it that you're so sure you're right
yet you keep restating everything
after your point's already made
what are you trying to prove,
that you're better?

what the hell are you talking about?
if I'm so great
why can't I understand
if I'm such a wonderful person
why do you have to keep telling me
if I'm so smart
why don't I know what I'm doing

why do you keep tormenting me
with your analysis of my greatness
if I'm so great
why would your words be of any use

if I'm the greatest friend
the most wholesome man
the smartest scholar
the wisest sage
why

why do I still NEED
why do I want
why do I feel
and why
why must I be convinced?

the heavy air

>
> the heavy air
> drains the energy from me
> the weight of the world
> rests on my shoulders
> drags me down
> into the dust
> to wrestle with
> the cockroaches and ants
> tearing my flesh with
> their jaws
> ingesting my body
> and laying their waste
> on the world

falling apart

> things are falling apart at the seams
> its all blowing up
> going to hell
> the debris of the days
> falls all around me
> the smoke rises and
> I cannot see
>
> is it death
> is it the end
> no, it's just life
> playing itself out
> like a tragic actor
> mortally wounded
> on stage
>
> I flip and flop
> like a fish on land
> trying to find water
>
> the ashes and embers of my life
> smolder on the ground
>
> soon I will rise like a phoenix
> whole again
> ready once more
> to die

PAIN AND DEATH

money for food

>
> explosion huge in my mind
> life
> the life I've known is collapsing
> leading to what
> the only place I've called home
> since the place I was raised in
> can no longer be mine
> I want to go
> but I must stay
> I don't know why
> this existence holds no future
> move on
> move on
> move
> but how
> I have no money
> I have no life
> I have nothing
> but my mind
> and isn't that enough
> the mind
> the source of existence
> if not for friends
> who inadvertently force me to stay
> I'd be a bum and wander the earth
> money for food
> everything else be damned
> damned
> damn this life
> of love
> and loss
> and hurt
> and death
> damn this death
> of life

perfectly happy

    hell can't be much worse than this
    heaven can't be much better
    with all the shit that goes on in my life
    I'm perfectly happy
    with all the pain and trouble
    I'm perfectly at ease
    people die
    people die
    people die every day and go on
    death and life are intertwined
    each the same as the other
    we all die a little every day
    and that's life
    as each day
    we inch closer
    to the grave

cross eyed world

    strike me hard
    slap me in the face
    till I can't see straight
    through crossed eyes

    shake me hard
    wake me up
    for only with eyes crossed
    can I see the cross world

    madness, anger, despair, & hurt
    covered with apologies & pretty phrases

    explain it to me then
    with your silver tongue
    that's never said or tasted anything
        bad
    let me see through those
    clear eyes of yours
    which have never seen sorrow

        YOU CAN'T

    sorrow & pain
    are the constants of the world
    more constant than the sun, moon, & stars
    which can be covered by clouds
    nothing can cover the agony of life
    as each day
    we die

mortality

    I don't understand
    I can't see it
    or hear it
    or feel it
    but something is there
    some thing in my life
    that I can't comprehend

    it is as if the specter of death himself
    were standing behind me
    glancing over my shoulder
    inspecting my work and life
    mortality

    is that what it is
    am I feeling my death today
    for the first time?

the mood strikes

    the mood strikes
    and I'm alone again
    in my own world
    with no one around
    but people

    every smile is a grimace
    that takes too much work
    my face is a mask
    upon which is etched
    the pain in my life

    pain from what
    I don't know
    its just pain

    pain from existing
    just from being alive
    the pain of being
    nothing

existence is pain

> the pain is reality
> the hunger in my belly
> reminds me that I need
> the eyes can deceive
> or go blind
> reality is not proven
> by sight or touch
> only the pain is real
> the pain is all
> existence is pain

I wish I could

> I wish I could catch
> a cool winter breeze
> and save it for a
> summer day
>
> I wish I could gather stars
> and give them to a
> black night
>
> I wish I could steal
> the shade from a tree
> and use it to guard
> my face from the burning sun
>
> I wish I could bury
> the pains in my life
> to hide them
> from the rest of the world

JOY AND LIFE

the fear of God

>   the eyes of God
>   look down upon me with
>   apprehension
>   in fear that I, in my
>   elation and this moment
>   of bliss will somehow
>   realize a fundamental
>   truth of life and become
>   a god and then will
>   have the power to set
>   things right, to destroy
>   evil itself and make the
>   world what it should be

anticipation soars

anticipation soars
and carries my mind away
on a trip I've yet to take
everything planned
and nothing known
so many things
to do
to see
to hear
to feel
in a world of chaos and pain
I search for something
the one truth to explain
existence
to seek it out
to hunt it down
and capture it
the truth of life
the truth of love

no direction

    driving in the eerie dark night
    down the lonely road
    like a bat out of hell
    who's going home to roost

    there is no plan
    no direction
    only the single driving consuming thought to
    go go go
    follow the road
    to nowhere

    I must go
    get out of this town
    away from the memories
    and lies
    away from the people
    away from life

    start anew
    believing nothing
    knowing nothing
    needing nothing
    but to go

driving through the night

    driving through the night
    trees passing unseen
    the road behind me
    disappearing into the darkness
    in the rear-view mirror
    and so is life
    experiences passing like trees
    and disappearing
    forgotten
    into the darkness
    of memory

Hardee's coffee

    Hardee's coffee
    Murray morning
    hard thoughts and short talk
    in low voices
    closing our ears
    to the country music coming
    from the jukebox

holy ground

    God

    you kneel
    you lift your hands
    you lower your eyes
    you speak in whispers
    you breathe

    you know nothing
    of God

    I do

    I know

    if God exists
    he's grown
    he's picked
    he's roasted
    ground
    brewed
    poured

    everyone looks for Him
    in the sky
    but I know
    he's in every cup
    of that dark
    holy
    liquid

coffee shop world

    strong bitter coffee
    slides easily down my throat
    I stare at the walls
    in awe
    Kerouac
    Ginsberg
    Einstein
    Davis
    the coffee shop world
    surrounds me
    as if in a dream
    but more real
    the table has substance
    the people have character
    the coffee tugs my brain
    into a whirl of thought
    as I breathe in the air
    the sounds
    of life

manic

    I suck down
    a cigarette
    as I suck
    my brain back
    through the holes
    in my head
    I get manic
    sometimes
    but I love it
    the energy
    the adrenaline rush
    from nothing other than
    my own
    activity

literati

>
> I'll take
> scruffy bearded bums
> with beer on their breath
> & cigarette stained fingertips
> over GQ geriatrics
> with bloated bellies &
> bloated stale old minds
> any day
> give me a bottle of
> Mickey's
> & a mike
> & I'll tell ya
> about life
> I'll tell ya

drunken poetry

> drunken poetry
> on beer bottle covered
> pool table
> pretty kitty
> asleep
> at corner pocket
> my head swims
> in the pool
> of beer drenched
> reality

overthrow

    I've got this plan, y'see
    I'm gonna take over the world
    with sound
    and orange & green peashooters
    no one shall oppose me
    not even the birds.

    oh, they'll fly
    and they'll twitter
    and flutter
    and poop
    but they'll not get me

    I will win
    and my prize will be
    a giant
    chocolate
    termite
    what can you say
    all you've got's an egg

    get out of my face
    go park your car
    I've got a world to rule
    and you've got jack
    Jack.

return to imperfection

ahhh…
adversity returns
pain returns
emotions return
life has returned
I feel the weight of the world
pressing down
and I love it
I smell the putrid swamp of life
as I breathe deeply
and I love it

a perfect world is not a right world
a perfect world can't be true
a perfect world sucks the marrow
from the dry bones of life

in a perfect world there's no thinking
there's no striving to set things right
it's the struggle that enlivens us
makes us who we are
and leads us down the road
to what we will
become

on edge

    things settle down
    my disturbed mind
    collects itself
    order from chaos
    descends
    and thoughts
    fly
    ideas images plans dreams
    whirl about
    toying with me
    on the edge
    of consciousness

the path

    they tried to tell me
    when I was younger
    that life is good
    they tried to explain
    about the nine-to-five
    that you actually like
    they tried to explain
    about the lovely young lady
    who'd always be by my side
    behind white picket fences
    and kitchen aprons
    and suckling little babies
    they tried to explain it
    even went so far as to
    try &
    prove it
    by living their lives like that
    for me

    it all seemed so simple
    the path so clear
    the choices life offered
    seemed so easily made
      school
        college
          work
              marry
            rear
          live
        die

    the path seemed so simple
    the choices so clear
    how is it that I've deviated?

    some sneaky mischievous prick
    somewhere along the line

must've flipped the signs
pointed me in the wrong direction
I stepped off the path
  got lost

I catch a glimpse every so often
through the undergrowth of life
  the path
I trudge through the brush & briars
recoiling from their annoying
sticks & scratches
trying so hard to
   MAKE IT
  back

I tried to tell myself
along the way
that my life is good
I tried to explain
that the choices I made
were right
I tried to explain
and the more I tried
the more I explained
the more I
   believed

the choices I've made
  ARE
and will stand
the only path I have to take
is the one I blaze
for myself

the world opens

    in the dark
    of deadest night
    rain falls
    and fills my cloudy head
    with visions of light
    and loveliness
    the world opened up
    to my eager eyes

    I get compliments from
    strange girls who say
      "you look so good now"
    and look at me with eyes
    regretful of past
      unnoticing
     moments
    eyes warm with ideas
    I no longer entertain
    even for a moment
    about them

    the world opens
    and my arms stretch
    sinewy & graceless
    to accept it
    in all its permutations
    of technicolor glory

    my legs twitch
    to run down roads
    with nothing at the end
    or in between
    to run to

    my mind holds fast to things I have
    and yearns for them
    and more

LOST POEMS

I want the world
in buckets
of love
  passion
    compassion
      endless nights
days
   hours
      minutes
time

time

    time time time
    moves too fast
    can't quite get a grip
    things happen
    with you
    or without
    what can ya do but
    tie yourself down
    & enjoy the ride

    time time
    it moves so slow
    it's easy to get
    impatient
    you want things to happen
    but they never do

    nothin's goin on
    nothin's happening
    it's at a standstill
    so just stand
    and laugh
    at the hurried wind

    time
    moves on its own
    can't kick it in the ass
    or grab it by the neck
    so just let it go
    and enjoy the moment
    or the moment
    will pass you by
    time is against you
    but time
    is on your side

now is the time

    we have a lot to discuss
    but now is not the time
    now we have to make the most
    of the time we've got
    now is not the time for worry
    now is not the time for doubt
    now is the time for us
    we can talk later
    but for now let's just
    live

invisible phantoms

    too much of life is
    invisible phantoms
    wafting through our days
    making things interesting
    enticing our minds
    our hearts and our souls
    to continue on
    no matter the cost
    personal or
    otherwise
    hope, dreams, love
    feelings, wants,
    NEEDS
    the intangibilities
    of existence
    impossible to grasp
    or define in concrete terms
    and yet so real
    in the disjointed logic
    of the mind
    so many things
    uncontrollable
    uncontainable
    but we continue to try
    catch hope and
    hold on
    define yr dreams
    love yrself
    and live

in the house of a stranger

    sitting comfortably
    in the house of a stranger
    hanging out with friends
    I don't know
    carrying on a conversation
    with one whose intelligence
    couldn't seem to cohabitate
    with his attitudes and actions
    new experiences around every corner
    never the same old thing
    and though I love the new
    the old has its attraction
    the familiarity of experiencing
    the same thing every year
    still, this is what I need
    new experiences
    new friends
    new thoughts
    new life

MATTHEW RASNAKE

what is left to write

    what is left to write
    as the poem of life passes by
    each person a verse
    each town a chapter
    in the epic of the world

    so many thoughts to think
    so many minds to open
    and read like a book

    do new and original thoughts exist
    or has everything been thought before
    does it matter

    as life feeds
    and death creeps
    we wander the pages
    and stroll through the streets of words
    adding punctuation as we go

    has someone walked this path before
    has this step been stepped
    has this leaf been blown
    or is the world always changing
    and always the same

LOST POEMS

her voice resounds

>high in the mountains
>the earth shifts
>under the weight of years
>deep in the granite of the world
>a pathway closes
>a subtle change
>and from that moment
>a quiet, cold mountain spring
>trickles into stillness
>this water, this source
>which has fed streams,
>creeks, and mighty rivers
>is ended
>
>but not silenced
>never silenced
>her voice will echo
>through all who've been touched by her
>
>her voice will resound
>through the valleys,
>   mountains,
>   canyons,
>   plains,
>and deserts of the world
>carried by those who sprang from her
>forever

in memory of Ruth
Feb 2 1916 – Jan 2 2009

beyond

the mountain beckons
the hills call
I sit alone among the trees
and listen to the hissing of the fire

the voices of the woods
whispering in my ear
the wind in the trees
the leaves rustle on the ground
and beyond it
is silence

away from the hustle bustle
of everyday life
away from people
there is only peace

nature is her own companion
she has no needs
beyond her own
existence.

ACKNOWLEDGMENTS

Countless family and friends have nurtured me throughout my life either physically, emotionally, or creatively and I owe all of them my gratitude.

Special thanks, of course, goes to my beautiful wife, Sara, my constant encourager and enabler, and the love of my life.

I'd also like to thank Dan, Sharon, and everyone else who bought or expressed interest in the limited editions of *the Christ of my Confusion*, the progenitor of this current work.

Undoubtedly, the bulk of this work wouldn't exist were it not for the creative crucible of my college years and the friendships that were forged there. Bob, Brax, Jim, Nathan, and Paul; Christiane, Jen, Jess, Kenny, Lori, and Wug; and later J. Brian too... you all were a big part of what I consider my second awakening.

And finally, from more recent times, I want to thank my patrons, who have contributed to and supported, both literally and figuratively, my work over the last year or so. Those honored friends are: Cori Dillahunty, Monroe & Flo (Mom and Dad) Rasnake, Javan Rasnake, Elizabeth Johnston, Chris Beck, Chris Gerstle, Steven & Ruthie Watson, Danny B, and Sharon Murphy. Your support and encouragement are so very appreciated.

www.ingramcontent.com/pod-product-compliance
Lightning Source LLC
Chambersburg PA
CBHW030915080526
44589CB00010B/313